# Jesus, I Adore You

*Thank you Blanche de C,*
*Anatole, Aristide and Achille B,*
*Prisca D and Marguerite L.*
*You've been my inspiration!*

by • bm

Under the direction of Romain Lizé, CEO, MAGNIFICAT
Editor, MAGNIFICAT: Isabelle Galmiche
Editor, Ignatius: Vivian Dudro
Proofreader: Kathleen Hollenbeck
Artistic Designers: Armelle Riva, Thérèse Jauze, Magali Meunier
Cover: Magali Meunier
Production: Thierry Dubus, Sabine Marioni

Original French edition: *Jésus, je t'adore*
© Mame, Paris, 2019

Sabine du Mesnil ✳ by • bm

# Jesus, I Adore You

### Children Praying
### before the Blessed Sacrament

MAGNIFICAT · Ignatius

# Contents

· PART 1 ·
## What Is Eucharistic Adoration?

A Meeting                                                             8
"Lord, where are you? My heart is looking for you!"                  10
"This is my Body."                                                   12
Come, Let Us Adore Him!                                              14
Source of Light and Life                                             16
"Blessed are the pure in heart,
for they shall see God!"                                             18


· PART 2 ·
## How Can I Adore God?

Prepare Your Heart for a Visit with Jesus!                           22
"Jesus, you are here!"                                               24
How Beautiful It Is to Keep Silent!                                  25
Being There                                                          26
Open the Door to Your Heart                                          28

## · PART 3 ·
## During Eucharistic Adoration

The Prayer of the Heart ........................................ 32

Little Signs from Heaven ...................................... 34

What a Racket! ..................................................... 36

"Lord, answer me!" .............................................. 38

God Works Wonders for Me! ................................ 40

What if I Fall Asleep? .......................................... 42

Helpful Hints ....................................................... 44

## · PART 4 ·
## Words of Adoration

In the Bible ......................................................... 48

Our Lady ............................................................. 54

Saint Francis ....................................................... 55

Saint Pio ............................................................. 56

Saint John Marie Vianney, the Curé of Ars ......... 57

Blessed Charles de Foucauld .............................. 58

Saint Augustine .................................................. 59

Saint Teresa of Calcutta ..................................... 60

Pope Benedict XVI ............................................. 61

"Jesus, I adore you!" ........................................... 62

# PART 1

# What Is Eucharistic Adoration?

# A Meeting

Jesus loves you! Every day he gives you, and all God's children, the gift of his presence. He has been here, right here in this world of ours, every day for more than two thousand years. We call Jesus Emmanuel, which means "God with us."

God is all-powerful. He could appear in a clap of thunder, surrounded by an army of angels. We would be dazzled by his beauty, and we would be scared of him! But instead, God speaks to us as a still, small voice like a gentle breeze. He cares for us as our Father. He is powerful in love. And so he chooses to become very small so that we can come close to him and see him without being afraid.

"*Lord, where are you?*
*My heart is looking for you!*"

In the quiet of a Catholic church we find a small, flickering red lamp. That shows us that Jesus is there, hidden in the tabernacle. The tabernacle is the beautiful cabinet near the altar. It reminds us of the tent in the desert where God came to meet Moses. The little flame tells us that behind the tabernacle door is the same God, in the form of Jesus made present in the Sacred Host. He is there day and night.

The risen Jesus promised us: "I am with you always, to the close of the age" (Matthew 28:20). Since ascending to heaven, Jesus has kept his promise every single day for more than two thousand years. He hasn't wanted to be separated from us for a single moment. What an extraordinary gift of love!

# "This is my Body."

At Mass, the priest says the words of Jesus: "This is my Body" and "This is the chalice of my Blood." At that moment, the bread and the wine become the Body and the Blood of Christ. With your eyes you can only see the Host and the Chalice, but with your mind and heart you believe that Jesus is there. Under the appearances of bread and wine, Christ is there before you. Jesus is really present with his divine life! What a mystery!

All those who receive Holy Communion receive Jesus, who is so great yet becomes so small, in the Host.

After Mass, the consecrated Hosts are placed lovingly in the tabernacle, like a treasure.

When he was a boy, Saint Peter Julian Eymard used to climb on a step ladder and lean his head against the tabernacle. He said, "I can hear him better like that." Jesus really is there, hidden in the tabernacle, and you can come close to him too.

*Jesus, Jesus,*
*my God, I adore you.*

# Come, Let Us Adore Him!

Sometimes, very reverently, the priest takes the Host out of the tabernacle for Exposition of the Blessed Sacrament. He places the Host in a beautiful container called a monstrance and sets it on the altar. Then everyone, grown-ups and children alike, can come and see Jesus. They can kneel and adore him.

Jesus is looking forward to your visit. He is waiting for you. Adoring him is a way of responding to his great love by paying him a little visit. Jesus is very happy when you come to visit him, simply, in silence.

In the church, God is waiting for you. You can go there and offer him your presence and your prayer. It's like throwing yourself into the arms of your heavenly Father, with trust and love.

# Source of Light and Life

"Eucharistic adoration is being there like a flower in front of the Sun," said Sister Marie-Therese of the Heart of Jesus. Imagine that flower: the sun's rays make its stem grow toward the sky and caress its petals… and then the flower opens up to the light.

You, too, can let God's light shine upon you.

And then, like the pollen that flies on the breeze, you can bring God's light to other people.

Eucharistic adoration is also a source of life, like a spring of clear water. On a hot summer day, how happy you are to have a drink of cold water! Well, adoration is like a drink of water for your heart, which is thirsty for love.

God is a spring of living, flowing water that never dries up. From him you can receive the love that fills you to overflowing and find love for other people too. Always.

*Whoever drinks of the water that I shall give him will never thirst; the water that I shall give him will become in him a spring of water welling up to eternal life.*

John 4:14

# Blessed are the pure in heart, for they shall see God!

(Matthew 5:8)

In adoration, God heals your impatience, anger, and jealousy. By adoring him you will become more like him. You will understand the wonderful things that the Lord is doing in your life, and you'll want to tell others about him!

You will learn to see Jesus more and more clearly in your father and mother, your brothers and sisters, and your grandparents, as well as the poor, the sick, or the people you find hard to love.

Adoring means seeing God and letting his presence shine out in the world.

# PART 2

# How Can I Adore God?

# Prepare Your Heart for a Visit with Jesus!

Going to a Holy Hour at your parish is like keeping an appointment with Jesus. You don't have to stay for the whole hour. Devoting ten minutes, a half hour, or however long you want to spend there is enough. Every visit makes Jesus happy.

When you have a close friend, you want to see that person and spend time with him or her. And you count the days and the hours before you can get together. When the time finally comes, you feel really happy! It's the same with Jesus. Look forward to meeting him in this time of adoration!

At what time will you go and see him? How long will you stay? What will you say to him? And what will he tell you?

> *Jesus, I offer you this time*
> *that I'm going to spend with you.*
> *Come, Holy Spirit, and prepare*
> *my heart for this meeting.*

# "Jesus, you are here!"

Jesus is there in the Host, and you come before him. In your heart, you can tell him,

> *You are here and you love me, Jesus!*
> *Thank you!*

When the Host is in a monstrance, you should go down on both knees and bow slightly at the waist, just like the Magi who knelt before Baby Jesus. You should also make a Sign of the Cross. With these gestures you are saying that God is there, present before you.

# How Beautiful It Is to Keep Silent!

When you go into the church to begin your Eucharistic adoration, keep silent. Silence is a prayer. In silence, we can hear the gentle breeze of God talking to us.

To help you listen to the silence, you can shut your eyes. Breathe slowly.

When you are calm and quiet, you are ready for your meeting with Jesus. And you can open your eyes again, slowly.

> *Jesus, here I am before you,*
> *simply, in silence.*
> *Nothing matters more to me*
> *than to live in your presence.*

# Being There

Adoration is very simple: all we have to do is be there, and that makes Jesus happy!

If kneeling is uncomfortable, sit down gently in a chair. You can also sit on the floor, on a carpet or a cushion. When you are quiet, you can receive and accept God's peace.

Don't forget: Jesus is happy when you draw near to him. His friend Saint John rested his head on Jesus's shoulder during the Last Supper. You too can rest tenderly on Jesus.

> *One of his disciples, whom Jesus loved,*
> *was lying close to the breast of Jesus.*
> John 13:23

Now lift your eyes to Jesus, present in the monstrance. Look at him... and let him look at you.

Adoration is a face-to-face meeting. Jesus is gazing at you. He looks at you happily because he loves you very much. Let his loving eyes touch your heart and lift your eyes to him. How happy God is when you look at him!

*Don't be afraid!*
*Let Christ look at you.*
*Let him look at you because he loves you.*

# Open the Door to Your Heart

Now you can talk freely to Jesus. You can tell him your joys, your sorrows, your secrets, and your worries, because you are talking to a friend.

The Lord loves to hear you talk to him. He is interested in everything you tell him.

You open your heart to the Lord, and he opens his to you. In that heart-to-heart talk, you can ask the Lord for what you desire for yourself, your family, your friends, and the whole world, and he will give to all whatever is good. The Spirit breathes between your heart and his, as a bond of love.

> *For where your treasure is,*
> *there will your heart be also.*
> Matthew 6:21

Your presence matters to Jesus.

If the time of adoration goes by slowly and you are eager to get back to your games, offer Jesus one little minute more: make him a gift of your presence.

Time spent with Jesus is never wasted, and you'll see how happy it makes you!

When you have finished, don't just rush out. Take the time to kneel down again and make the Sign of the Cross carefully to say goodbye to Jesus.

You can also promise him to come back. Will it be next week? In a month's time? What matters is that you are faithful to the appointment you make with Jesus!

# PART 3

# During Eucharistic Adoration

# The Prayer of the Heart

Sometimes adoration is very easy: you find that it's good to be there with Jesus, and you are happy to spend time with him.

Sometimes it's more difficult: you can't see Jesus, you can't hear him, and so you are not too sure what to say to him.

If you don't know what to do, here are some ideas to help you.

Don't worry: even if you don't feel anything, Jesus is there, close to you, and he loves you!

If you don't know how to talk to Jesus, let Jesus talk to you, through God's Word. Find a sentence in the Bible that means something to you. Repeat it again and again until you can say it by heart. Then it turns into a sort of tune that plays inside you.

One day, perhaps, it will come into your mind and you'll feel God's presence, his strength, at your side.

> *Your words were found, and I ate them,*
> *and your words became to me a joy*
> *and the delight of my heart.*
>
> Jeremiah 15:16

# Little Signs from Heaven

Sometimes it's hard to concentrate during adoration. Are you starting to look around you? Don't worry. On the altar and all around, you can see things that will help you to turn to God again.

You can admire the monstrance that holds Jesus in the Host. It is like a jewel or a sunburst. Its shining rays surround Jesus and come forth from him. He is our most precious treasure. He is like the sun, which warms your heart and lights up the whole world.

On the altar and in other parts of the church, lots of candles are burning. They are a sign of the presence of God, the Light of the world. Jesus is the Light, the one who guides you through the night. It is Jesus who helps you feel safe when you are afraid and warms you when you are feeling cold. Ask Jesus to come and shed his light on you.

Can you see the little stand that hold up the monstrance? It's called a tabor. Tabor was the name of the mountain in Galilee where Jesus was transfigured and three of his apostles saw him shining with radiant light. Mount Tabor was where they met Jesus in his glory; and the little tabor on the altar is where you can meet Jesus today. Are you ready?

Did you know that a whole crowd of angels are adoring God with you? They are there, close to you, even though you can't see them.

*I heard around the throne... the voice of many angels, numbering myriads of myriads and thousands of thousands.*
Revelation 5:11

# What a Racket!

Sometimes thoughts jostle together in your head, and you don't seem to be thinking about Jesus at all. You might be thinking about the racetrack you're building for your toy cars, the birthday party you will be attending next week, the quarrel you had with your brother or sister, and lots of other things!

Don't worry. Tell Jesus about all these things right now. He's interested in you and everything you're thinking about! Talk to him about the things that make you happy and the things that make you sad.

Don't be afraid. Jesus loves you the way you are, with your doubts, your faults, and your good qualities too.

*You are precious in my eyes... and I love you...*
*Fear not, for I am with you.*

Isaiah 43:4-5

# "Lord, answer me!"

All around you, there are people suffering from illness, loneliness, and conflicts. You've asked God for help. Perhaps you are feeling discouraged because God doesn't seem to be answering your prayers.

God will not always give you what you ask for in the way you expect. Prayer is not a magic spell! But you have to keep trusting. God wants you to be truly happy, and he will always give you what you need. Sometimes what you need is the strength to handle bad things that happen, and God will give you that. God is close to you; he is your loving Father.

> *Your Father knows what you need before you ask him.*
>
> Matthew 6:8

Sometimes at adoration you don't feel anything at all! You doubt God is really there. So why bother going to visit Jesus, you might think. That's when you need to remember that even great saints, such as Saint Teresa of Calcutta, also known as Mother Teresa, had times of darkness, times when God felt far away. Yet they remained faithful: they kept praying, every single day. Whenever you doubt, trust that God loves you. Even when it's hard, stay faithful to Eucharistic adoration. Although we don't always feel close to God, time spent with him in prayer is always fruitful.

*He who abides in me, and I in him,*
*he it is that bears much fruit.*

John 15:5

# God Works Wonders for Me!

In Jesus's presence, think about the good things in your life. What nice things happened to you today? Or this week? This year? Since you were born? Take time to remember, with Jesus, all the good things he has done for you and with you. See how much he loves you. Then ask Jesus to help you see the good things in your life that you have forgotten. Jesus will help you remember; he has been by your side all along!

Thank Jesus for your family, for all the gifts he has given you, and even for those he hasn't given you yet!

*I will not forget you.*
*Behold, I have graven you on the palms of my hands.*
                                                    Isaiah 49:15-16

The sun shining in the sky
A hug from my mother
A game with my father
A good grade at school
A walk in the forest
My friends
The good priests at my parish
My baby sister's smile
My grandparents
A pretty flower

...

# What if I Fall Asleep?

Don't worry if you fall asleep. When you wake up, Jesus will still be there, with his heart wide open to you. He's watching over you, as he always does. Even when you're asleep, he still loves you.

(That doesn't mean you should bring a pillow with you to Eucharistic adoration! Like any friend, God is happy when you come and talk with him.)

*He gives to his beloved sleep.*
Psalm 127:2

# Helpful Hints

Before you visit Jesus, make a list of the things you would like to tell him. You might list your heart's desires, things that have made you sad, reasons to be thankful, and people who need prayers. Then when you go to Eucharistic adoration, you can take the list and read it to Jesus!

Ask your mother or father for your own notebook. After Mass, write in your notebook anything you heard that encouraged you, inspired you, or made you think, "This is Jesus speaking to me today!" Take the notebook with you to adoration and read over those words.

Think of someone in your class who doesn't know Jesus very well. Pray for him or her during Eucharistic adoration. Perhaps it will lead to a wonderful conversation. And–Who knows?–that person may come with you to adoration some time!

Learn a joyful hymn of praise. You can sing it under your breath, telling Jesus again and again how much you love him.

# PART 4

# Words of Adoration

# In the Bible

*I have calmed and quieted my soul,*
*like a child quieted at its mother's breast.*

Psalm 131:2

A small child rests in his mother's arms. He is close to his mother's heart, and she rocks him gently. He can feel how much he is loved!

Just like that, in adoration, you are close to Jesus's heart and can leave your fears behind. You are like a small child in God's arms, and your heart is at rest.

God of tenderness, we praise you!

*I will rejoice and be glad for your merciful love.*
Psalm 31:7

God loves you just as you are–with every single one of your good qualities and every single one of your weaknesses. Don't be afraid to ask him to help you when you feel sad. You will see how happy it makes you to be loved by God exactly as you are!

Then you will feel like dancing for joy! Even the great King David, in the Bible, started to dance when the Ark of the Covenant entered Jerusalem. He was delighted to know that God was with him all the days of his life!

*The LORD is my shepherd,*
*I shall not want;*
*he makes me lie down in green pastures.*

Psalm 23:1-2

A shepherd guides his sheep to what is best for them: green grass, shade, and water. The Lord takes care of you just like that; you have no need to fear. He watches over you and guides you. You can trust him because he wants you to be truly happy. You are like his little lamb.

*This is my body*
*which is given for you.*
Luke 22:19

At Communion, the wafer of bread in front of you is really the Body of Christ. Jesus offered himself for you on the Cross. He died and rose from the dead for you. At each Mass, at his words, the bread becomes his Body. At Eucharistic adoration, the Host in the monstrance is really Christ. You are looking at God.

*You shall love the LORD your God
with all your heart,
and with all your soul,
and with all your might.*

Deuteronomy 6:5

The first of the Ten Commandments, to love God with all your heart, is a prayer said by Jewish people every day. They learn it by heart, and whole families say it together from sunrise to sunset–even the youngest! They say it when traveling, and they place it beside the doors of their homes. Jesus prayed this prayer too. He said that these words make up the greatest of all the commandments. It is a good prayer for you to repeat during Eucharistic adoration. It will write itself on your heart, helping you to love God more and more.

*Let the children come to me, do not hinder them;*
*for to such belongs the kingdom of God.*

Mark 10:14

Jesus blesses children and waits for them with his arms wide open! When he is present at adoration, he is waiting for you! Don't be afraid; draw near to him.

# Our Lady

Mary said yes when the angel told her that she would give birth to Jesus, the Son of God. Her heart was overflowing with happiness. She ran to tell the news to her cousin Elizabeth and called out:

> *He who is mighty has done great things for me,*
> *and holy is his name.*

Luke 1:49

Here on earth, Mary carried Jesus in her arms. She fed him, loved him, and thought about him for thirty-three years! So now, at each Mass and each adoration, she is there. She is close to her Son, and close to us.

Mary, help me to love Jesus! Make him grow in me! Help me to see all the great things that Jesus does in my life!

# Saint Francis

Saint Francis of Assisi lived in Italy, between the twelfth and thirteenth centuries. He had great love for Jesus Christ. And he adored him in the Blessed Sacrament.

Saint Francis once said:

*What wonderful majesty, what amazing kindness!*
*For the Lord of the universe*
*to humble himself like this*
*and hide under the form*
*of a little bread!*
*Humble yourselves, make yourselves little,*
*that you may be raised up by him.*

Jesus makes himself little and humble in order to meet us. In adoration, he is there in front of us, and we can offer him our hearts in this prayer:

Jesus, you are here, quite simply, in front of me. Help me to stay humble and little in front of you, because you come to meet me. Thank you!

# Saint Pio

Saint Pio, often called Padre Pio, was a Capuchin monk and priest in southern Italy. Like Saint Francis of Assisi, he received on his body the marks called stigmata. He was so close to Jesus that he shared in his sufferings on the Cross in order to change men's hearts.

Padre Pio prayed:

*Yes, Jesus, I love you and I feel the need to love you even more; but, Jesus, I haven't got any more love left in my heart. You know that I've given it all to you. If you want more love, take my heart and fill it with your love, and then command me to love you. Please, do this, grant my desire. Amen.*

Sometimes it's quite hard to love. Your heart feels empty like a well that is dry! God, who is total love, can fill your heart with love.

"Come, Lord, into my heart!"

# Saint John Marie Vianney,

## THE CURÉ OF ARS

Saint John Marie Vianney is the patron saint of all the priests in the world. He spent hours hearing confessions and praying in front of the Blessed Sacrament. He would point to the tabernacle and say, "He's there, he's there, in the sacrament of his love."

This holy priest prayed:

> *I love you, O my God,*
> *and my only desire*
> *is to love you*
> *to the very last moment of my life.*

Close to Jesus in the Blessed Sacrament, you're not afraid of anything.

Do you want to stay closely united to him this week? Tell him again and again, "I love you. Stay with me, Lord!"

# Blessed Charles de Foucauld

Charles de Foucauld was a soldier at first, and he lived his life far from God. But one day he fell in love with Jesus. He moved to the North African desert, where he humbly served the people who lived there and spent many hours praying before the Blessed Sacrament. He often meditated on the words Jesus spoke on the Cross.

Blessed Charles de Foucauld prayed:

*O God my Father,*
*I abandon myself to you.*
*Do whatever you want with me.*
*Whatever you do with me,*
*I will thank you.*
*I give my soul into your hands.*
*I give it to you, my God,*
*with all the love of my heart…*
*because you are my Father.*

You can make this prayer your own by saying, "Help me, Jesus, to accept whatever life brings and to do whatever God asks with love and complete trust in the Father."

# Saint Augustine

Saint Augustine was born in North Africa in the fourth century. He was very intelligent. He looked for God in many different ways, and after a long time he found him, speaking to his own heart! Later Saint Augustine became the bishop of Hippo. He is known as a Doctor of the Church and one of the Fathers of the Church.

Saint Augustine told God:

> *You have made us for yourself,*
> *and our heart is restless*
> *until it rests in you.*

You might be looking for God. Simply ask him, "God, where can I find you?" Sometimes it's noise that keeps us from God, and sometimes it's doubt. So go into your heart, in silence. God is there. You will find him, the one who has loved you since before you were born: God, the only one you can't live without!

# Saint Teresa of Calcutta

Mother Teresa was a nun who founded the Missionaries of Charity in India. She looked after people nobody cared about–street children, the homeless, the dying. She saw the face of Jesus in each of them. As the leader of her community she decided to hold one hour of Eucharistic adoration every day. She and her sisters found that they had more time than before and more love with which to serve the poor.

Mother Teresa said:

> *Jesus is my God.*
> *Jesus is my Spouse.*
> *Jesus is my Life.*
> *Jesus is my only Love.*
> *Jesus is my All in All.*
> *Jesus is my Everything.*

And I too, kneeling before Jesus in adoration, come to draw from him the strength to smile, serve, love, and console people. Help me, Jesus, to see you in each of my family members, friends, and the people around me.

# Pope Benedict XVI

Pope Benedict XVI visited Lourdes, France, on September 14, 2008. With thousands of pilgrims, he adored Jesus in a Eucharistic procession.

He said:

*Lord Jesus, you are here!*
*And you, my brothers, my sisters, my friends,*
*you are here, with me, in his presence!*
*We contemplate him.*
*We adore him.*
*We love him.*
*We seek to grow in love for him.*

With the whole Church, we meet Jesus in the Eucharist. Together, we adore him, and so the love between us grows.

Jesus, teach me, together with my brothers and sisters, to contemplate you and to see your face in all those around me. Stay with me all the days of my life.

# "Jesus, I adore you!"

Adoring means "being there" close to Jesus. Like Jesus. Just there, present.

Do you want to become a person who brings love, peace, and joy to the world? The world needs it so much!

Come and draw love, peace, and joy from the heart of Jesus. He is waiting for you! Come and find him, come and adore him!

*I'm coming to you, Jesus.*

I am going to Eucharistic adoration

on

..........................................................................................................................

from

..........................................................................................................................

to

..........................................................................................................................

at the church of

..........................................................................................................................

Printed in November 2020, in Poland, by Dimograf.
Job number MGN21005
Printed in compliance with the Consumer Protection Safety Act, 200